# The Drum

*A step-by-st*ep guide to b*c*o*me a s*uccessful, *competitive drum major.*

### Halei Jo Fuller

I would like to thank Mr. Kyle Snavely, Mr. Francis Franqui, Mr. Jeffrey Willis, Emily Baker, and my parents—Joe and Shelly Fuller—who have taught me so much about being a better musician, a better person, and a better leader. Thank you for all that you do. This book is dedicated to you.

# Contents

# Introduction

*"We have begun a new era. We are part of something really special and you may not know it yet, but it's going to be monumental. Let's rehearse like champions!"*

—my band director, Mr. Francis Franqui,
August 2011

Going above and beyond what is required is the best way to approach any job. The drum major position requires much of your time—you have to be willing to put all of your heart and soul into what you are doing, your blood, sweat, and tears. This isn't an easy position, but if you are willing to work, you will have the time of your life. Going above what is expected...is expected. Are you willing to accept this challenge? If you're thinking about it, this book will give you an idea of what it takes and how to do it.

Many behind-the-scenes obstacles pop up during rehearsals, football games, and competitions. You won't figure out how to solve these problems on a website, in books, or in leadership pamphlets, and I promise that you have never seen some of them. Some of the skills you need to handle these situations are not taught; they are learned on the spot.

You must learn to trust your instincts. -You cannot fail, and you will not fail. This handbook will help you learn to trust your instincts and handle these situations.

Questions to ask yourself before considering becoming a drum major:

- Are you willing to dedicate most of your free time to band?
- Are you willing to clean the band room every day after school?
- Are you willing to grow up? (Don't deny that you need to...)
- Are you willing to lose your (untrue) friends?
- Are you willing to accept responsibility for things that might not even be your fault?
- Are you willing to accept the mistakes you will make? (Yes, you are human.)
- Are you willing to volunteer for everything band-related?
- Are you willing to arrive to every band event first and leave it last?
- Are you willing to accept even the most difficult of tasks?
- Are you willing to be strong even in the most difficult situations?
- Are you willing to not be dramatic?
- Are you willing to talk to everyone and be friendly?
- Are you willing to go the extra mile in everything you do in your life?
- Are you willing to set the example?

## The Basics

The classic everyday duties of a drum major are as follows:
- Attend all band functions.
- Be responsible to the director for the conduct and actions of the band at all times, and for the execution of all band duties assigned.
- Take charge of band in all types of situations.
- Assist the director in maintaining discipline and order.
- Assist the director with marching drill, inspection, planning, and special activities.
- Promote band standards and pride.
- Attend all band council meetings.
- Coordinate and supervise all section leaders and be responsible for their effectiveness and actions.
- Ensure all rehearsals begin on time.
- Ensure that at the end of an evening rehearsal the facility is locked up and clean.
- Organize staff books with music and drill for every rehearsal.

You may want to memorize these bullet points for your audition. However, these points only skim the surface of everything that goes into being a successful drum major. Those are the basics; this handbook will teach you how to make sure those eleven duties get done and, more important, how they get done right.

Question: Why are you a good candidate for this position? What do you offer to make your program better? What makes you special?

# Chapter 1: The Five Most Important Rules for Being a Drum Major

## Rule 1—Never Ask Questions

Use your brain: you know what the answer is. Your director has given you a task to do, whether it be answering a one-word question or finishing a multistep to-do list. Your job is to do this task as quickly and as well as possible. Your director is already dealing with enough—he or she doesn't need another question. There have been so many times when I have had to give directions to the band and either I didn't hear the director or I simply had to make the call on my own. Trust your instincts: 88 percent of the time you will be right, and when you are not, well just go with it. Most of the time the director will appreciate the effort to make his or her life easier.

## Rule 2—Believe in Yourself

Not once has a well-known leader shown self-doubt in front of someone. Everyone has doubts, but as a leader; we can *never* show them.

Whether it be conducting, giving a command, or just making a statement, you should believe in what you are doing with all of your heart. If you don't fully believe in yourself, than no one will believe in you. No one will take you seriously.

First think about what you are going to say and *then* say it. Sometimes it takes me ten seconds to think of the right thing to say, but at least I say the right thing confidently. However, this is usually something you have to do on the spot, so think fast! Making announcements isn't easy. Standing in front of two hundred people isn't easy, but it's something you have to do. If you look nervous, people won't believe in you. If you are obviously afraid, people won't see you as a leader but just a person standing in a position without fulfilling the role.

For example, when you're conducting, people will enjoy it if you get into the music (if you're expressive). Be the music—feel it and embody it. You portray what the music has to say through the way you conduct. I've gotten many compliments on my conducting because I believe in what I am doing. I never laugh at myself and say, "Jeez, what am I doing?" Of course, there's a boundary there—you aren't Gustavo Dudamel conducting the LA Phil: you are a drum major, and the most important thing is a *clear* beat pattern!

Reflection: List some instances in which you have doubted yourself and explain why. Then, come up with solutions to avoid revisiting that situation.

### Rule 3—Be Strong

There will be people who are jealous of you; your family may get upset because you are

never home, and yes you do get criticized—
you get criticized a lot.

It takes a strong-minded and equally
strong-hearted person to be a drum major.
You have to make many decisions on your
own, and those decisions may not always be
right. Plus you cannot please everyone—it is
simply impossible. You cannot beat yourself
up about it, you must, *must* move on. Don't
think twice about it. If the band sees you in a
vulnerable state, you are being
unprofessional. You must be strong; you can
cry or punch a pillow when you are alone, if
you have to.

Never let issues get bottled up inside of
you. If something is so bad that it is eating
you away, vent to someone. Just make sure
you pick the right person or it will backfire on
you. Perhaps someone who doesn't go to your
school, or someone that is not in your band.

As a drum major, you take the blame
for just about everything. Be prepared: if one
freshman saxophone player doesn't have his
or her dot card, it's your fault. Why? Well, you
are responsible for making sure the section
leaders have dot cards. Why not make sure
you *and* the horn captains have an extra set?
It's the higher-level thinking, the "what if…"
Therefore, even if it wasn't your fault, it is—it
always is. If someone never brings water to
rehearsal, it's your fault. If someone forgets
his or her gloves, it's your fault. If someone
yawns at attention; it's your fault. If
operations forgot something, it's your fault.

Even if you think the problem has no relation to you at all, it will always be the drum major's fault because it *does* relate to the drum major—*always*. It takes some time to get used to this. As a DM, you take a lot of grief.

This year, I took the blame for different things that happened because explaining what had happened was simply a waste of time. (While you are telling the story about what happened, you could have been running back to the band room to get the item that was forgotten in the first place.) Don't get upset at being blamed for everything: it's part of your job. Also, throwing one of your colleagues under the bus is evidence of weakness and a quality of a poor leader.

As far as "haters" go—they despise you no matter what. You took their spot when you became drum major, you proved them wrong about something, you have too many friends, you are a better musician—it could be anything. The simplest advice I can give you is to not think twice about it. I have been there. It really feels bad, but you have to suck it up and be strong. There are so many people that love and appreciate you—focus on what you have and you will feel a lot better. Take the hatred as a compliment. You must be doing something right.

## Rule 4—Take the Initiative

Never waste time. Never wait for someone else to do something. Never wait for something to get resolved or for the weather to clear up before you get something done. Never let someone tell you what you can or cannot do. Never let people doubt you or think for a moment that they cannot rely on you. Always be the first to volunteer. Be the one that everyone can come to with anything. Always accept the challenge at hand. Always think of ways to be efficient with your time. Don't let a minute pass by at rehearsal when you are not doing something beneficial.

If someone needs to run back to the band room, don't stand there and stare at one another. *YOU* go run; don't think twice about your decision. Be the person that anyone can come to with anything knowing it will get done right and as quickly as possible. Taking the initiative is a way of life; the most successful people in this world use this skill. If there is trash on the floor, are you going to go find someone and ask him or her to pick it up? No, of course not: you are going to pick it up. It takes triple the time to ask someone to pick trash up off the floor than to just do it yourself. It's the same story with just about everything.

Question: What are ten tasks you can think of that would be done more efficiently if you take the initiative?

1.

2.

3.

4.

5.

6.

7.

8.

9.

10.

## Rule 5—Delegate

Taking the initiative is very important, but another aspect of being a drum major is being able to delegate work to others. You simply can't do everything on your own, and if you try, you will have a mental breakdown. You will be putting way too much pressure on yourself.

Delegating tasks isn't just a way to avoid overworking yourself—it is also a way to be more efficient. Your overall objective is to make sure tasks get done as smoothly and quickly as possible. Asking others to help out shortens the amount of time it takes to complete your to-do list. But be cautious *who* you ask, and constantly check up on them to make sure the job you assigned is getting done efficiently and correctly.

When you delegate, *ask* for help. **Do not tell someone to do something**. You earn respect this way. When you *ask* people for help, it makes them feel more important to the organization, and in return they will have higher confidence and want to work harder. If you *tell* or *order* people to do something, that makes them bitter and creates negative feelings toward you. Think about it: when are you more likely to do something your parents need from you? When they ask you to do it, or when they tell you to? Everyone wants to feel important. Asking does that. Telling belittles people because it's a form of talking down to them.

Delegation is not only important with the band but it is equally, if not more, important with your section. As the drum major section, it is your responsibility to make sure everything of any importance at all gets done. You have to split your work—this way no one will feel overloaded or unimportant. Have a weekly meeting, and decide who does what on which nights.

It's a balancing act: initiative versus delegation. Which one is more effective? You must balance them out. Don't be the DM who demands that everyone else do tasks and who doesn't help out (the disease known as extreme delegationitis), and don't be the DM who does everything alone (extreme

initiativitis). Meet somewhere in the middle.
About 20 percent more weight should be on
the initiative side, though.

Question: What are ten tasks that would be
completed more efficiently with delegation?

1.

2.

3.

4.

5.

6.

7.

8.

9.

10.

# CHAPTER 2: REHEARSALS

In this chapter, I offer a quick guide to how your rehearsals should go and what to watch out for.

## Basic Rehearsal Schedule

1. **Stretch band.** *Never take longer than five minutes*! The band should be allowed to speak during this time as long as members are still stretching. It's the last time they will get to talk for three hours.
2. **Basics. Th**e *visual staff run basics for hal*f an hour to an hour. Be there for whatever they need. Tell one of them everytime five minutes passes , he or she may want you conducting or gocking a tempo. If not, this is the perfect time to *run* (not walk) to the band room to get something that was forgotten or that the director needs.
3. **Music Warm-up.** Your director runs this section of rehearsal. It can last from fifteen to forty-five minutes. You must be with*in the* director's line of sight at all times. You will be requested to conduct a part of the show.
4. **Drill.** During an average rehearsal, the second hour is when the band learns drill. This means you keep up rehearsal etiquette and conduct. *Never zone out*.

Always be on your game and *be prepared for anything*.
5. **Segments.** Usually the last hour of rehearsal is when the band segments the show, a time for extreme concentration. This is the final push toward having a great rehearsal; it's the make-or-break moment.

This is classically when band begins to get tired and talk—this is your biggest time to control and correct etiquette. Keep in mind you will be tired too, but you can't let that stop you from doing your job correctly. It is imperative that you stay aware of what is happening around you at all times.

**Rehearsal Etiquette**

If your hands are up, the band's instruments are up as well. When you put your hands down, their instruments go down and the staff gets to say what they need to say. When you say "set," the staff time is over. Give the directions the tower told you to give. If anyone isn't at set with instruments at a carry, bring your hands down and repeat. Once everyone is in the loop, tell the band the set number that the box told you and bring hands to conducting position. The band shall then bring instruments to playing position. Eight clicks from the met and the set begins.

If there is talking on the field, catch it before it gets out of control. Talking is like a virus that spreads insanely fast. If you let one person get away with it, then others will begin to speak because they see that person wasn't called out for it.

In order to stop the talking, *never* yell, "Stop talking!" That statement is the world's most annoying thing to hear, and it doesn't solve the problem. *Always* call out a specific name or section. This is when people start to take you seriously—no one wants to be called out by name.

As hard as it may seem, don't let your friends off on these rules. Rules are rules: you can be the nicest, most bestest friend off the field, but when you are at rehearsal, you have to be the rule enforcer. You can be friendly with people. I'm not telling you, you can't have friends at rehearsal—I'm simply saying be prepared to not always be a friend. This job isn't about making new friends all of the time. There are some boundaries, and if people are not happy with what you decide, you can always talk to them after rehearsal about it. It isn't your job to make sure everyone loves you. It is your job to make sure rehearsal always goes really well.

## Your Backpack

Every drum major must bring a backpack to rehearsal carrying *everything*. Think of anything that could go wrong and be prepared to tackle the challenge.

Here's what should be in your backpack. An asterisk (*) denotes items that will ruin a rehearsal if missing:

- At least 3 sets of extra drill*
- Music binder (1" white binder with clear plastic cover on front)*
- Cheat sheet (will be covered later on)
- Extra score binder(1" flexible colored binder)
- Batteries*
- Mini metronome*
- Earbud headphones for mini metronome
- Extra black towel for brass player
- Extra gloves for brass
- Reeds
- Baritone mouthpiece
- Valve oil
- Flashlight
- Mini first-aid kit
- Pencils
- Sharpie
- Highlighter
- Duct tape
- Stick/guard tape
- Drum key
- Gock block and drumstick*
- **Extra** set of drumsticks and extra gock block
- Paper clips (for drill—*and* you never know when a paper clip will come in handy for fixing instruments, light key, picking locks—you would be surprised.)

- Two extra bottles of water for the kid who ran out of water
- Watch*
- Rubber bands (for broken instruments and dot cards)
- Notebook to write long tasks down or mini notes
- Extra hat
- Extra sunglasses
- Hair ties
- Extra T-shirt for when it rains
- White gloves, white gloves, and more white gloves
- Black T-shirt*
-

Credit: Mr. Kyle Snavely

Believe it or not, my band used all of these items at least once this past season.

## Items You Need That Don't Fit in a Backpack

- Dr. Beat—make sure the "doctor" is set because if not, your career is over
- Extra batteries for Dr. Beat in the Long Ranger case (yes, they should *also* be in your backpack)
- The handheld microphone (goes on tower plugged in and ready for director)
- Speaker system (by the pit under the tower)
- Extension cords (for the speaker system)

- Long Ranger—another item that being without can end your career
- Long Ranger tripod
- Ladders/podiums
- Wireless mic for staff during basics
- Cones or whatever yard line marker your program uses.
- Chalk(if on pavement)
- Dot cards/dot books

Question: What can you do to remind yourself to bring all of these items? Is there anything else you can think of that you need for your program?

## Tasks to Complete *Before* Rehearsal Begins

- Give the staff a gock block and stick for basics. Sometimes the guard needs one as well, so always have at least four between all of the DMs.
- Print and copy *drill* for staff. This year I went ahead and made three drill binders just so the staff would always have an organized set of drill to look at. This helps because people don't lose it and you don't have to print out as many copies.
- Be ready to get anything the staff asks from you.
- Find out what the director and staff are planning to do during rehearsal *before*

rehearsal so you can have a schedule already planned out in your mind.

- Always have spare music scores and drill for the director as well! Keep the extras in a folder in your backpack or make more extra binders to have on hand.

## What Needs to Happen During Rehearsal

- During basics always check time and signal visual staff every five to ten minutes (whatever they request)
- Always have a set of keys to unlock bathroom doors, get into the band room, open storage closets, and so on.
- Time management—keep up the speed at which people are moving back to their previous set. Also make sure you give directions as quickly and in as straightforward a manner as possible.
- Keep everyone fully engaged. Say "yay!" once in a while! A good attitude is a way better rehearsal from start to finish.
- Keep rehearsal etiquette perfect. If you let one person speak, it's going to snowball out of control. Never call out a whole section for just one person— always use the person's name directly. This stops talking quickly and efficiently. This also works with calling for horns up and down, set, attention, and so on. *Be relentless.*

- Always have your phone on you. Contact is extremely important between director and drum majors.

Question: How do you want your rehearsal run? What would you do to make sure it goes the way you want it to go?

**Percussion Rehearsal**

Your job during this rehearsal is to either run the metronome, follow the drum line with the Long Ranger, conduct, or—most important— listen and learn. This is the perfect time to really learn the different segments of the show! You can make out checkpoints with the drum line's "hits" or "impacts" and their relationship with the winds(in your head, of course—they aren't at this rehearsal).

Need for drum line rehearsal
- Score binder
- Water
- Hat/sunglasses

Your responsibility at percussion rehearsal is much less important than at a regular rehearsal. The line's operations team is responsible for the met and Dr. Beat. You will usually show up when they begin segmenting. Just make sure that during these rehearsals you are paying close attention because it will help immensely when the whole band is in rehearsal and you accidentally forgot the set the band was ending at. *Know the music.*

## Time Management

It is your responsibility to make sure that everything happens *before* it is scheduled to happen.

If your call time is 4:00, you should have the band at attention at 3:58. Chances are, the director's watch is fast, and if it's not, well it's always nice to be safe and ahead of schedule.

Rehearsal: **If you gock your band out to your rehearsal location**, you should meet up with your band in the scheduled location. and leave fifteen minutes prior to rehearsal. I recommend marching at a pace at around 130 bpm so you are not wasting any time. (When you gock, have a metronome plugged into a headset in one ear). Once there, give the band a warning every few minutes. At five minutes before rehearsal begins, have people move to their warm-up area(s). This season, I always told members rehearsal was going to start in two minutes even if it was really five so they would hurry to where they needed to be. It's always a bonus when your director gets to rehearsal, if he or she is not already there, and you are stretching three minutes before the official start of rehearsal. In a director's eyes, that is on time, and it should be in your eyes as well as the rest of the organization's.

**If you do not gock your band to your rehearsal, ignore the first section of the above paragraph and start with the warning to take positions.**

*The following description of rehearsal is how my band's rehearsals are scheduled—change whatever you need to.*

Start in two arcs (brass behind woodwinds). Point to the ends of the arc and the members should begin to ripple down to a squat to retrieve a sip of water and set their instruments down. Give them a few seconds and then point to the center, and they will ripple back up and out. Have everyone spread out and then lead the stretching—make sure it is never more than five minutes long. Have fun with it; get the group pumped for the amazing rehearsal they are about to have! Afterward get everyone in the arcs again and let the director take over for music warm-up.

During music warm-up always stand off to the side, watching and listening. You will learn a lot by watching the director conduct the show, and you will be called to conduct segments as well. Have your music binder with you, a gock block/drumstick, and your water.

After music warm-up, the visual staff takes over for marching basics and/or different exercises. Basics can last anywhere from thirty minutes to an hour. During this time it is your job to tell the visual staff how much time they have every ten minutes or so.

Sometimes they need you to conduct as well, and most of the time, you will be gocking a tempo for them. Just be on watch at all times. This is also a great opportunity to run back to the band room if something has been forgotten.

Question: What will you do to make sure you are always *ahead* of schedule? How are your rehearsals run?

# Your Rehearsal Schedule

# CHAPTER 3: PERFORMANCES

## Football Games

Football games are all about maintaining a professional environment and also having fun. It's hard to maintain balance between these two actions, but as a drum major, it is imperative you do. You must watch out for unprofessional behavior the whole, entire game—whether it be playing with bad tone quality or just acting stupid. You have to control it. This is high school, and yes football is super exciting, but if you let people act like idiots, what does that accomplish? (It proves the stereotype of a band geek, duh!)

Another aspect of a football game is making sure everything you need gets to the stadium!

Do not forget the wireless microphone and Long Ranger.
*Do not forget the wireless microphone and Long Ranger.*
**Do not forget the wireless microphone and Long Ranger.**

If you forget the wireless microphone and/or the Long Ranger at a football game, the band cannot hear what the director is saying. It's mass hysteria—no one knows what stands tunes/songs and where they are as far as defense/offense. The whole night becomes an unorganized mess. So remember to bring those two items or assign someone to bring them (delegate) and check with that person before every game.

Need for a Football Game
- Wireless microphone
- Long Ranger
- Long Ranger tripod (optional)
- Gloves
- Medicine bag

## Competitions

One word: *professionalism*. Make sure no one acts out of character. At competitions, it is uncommon for people to misbehave—most people are completely focused under pressure—but if they do, you have to stop them immediately. It is distracting and puts a bad taste in everyone's mouth. Because of the desire to win, it shouldn't be too difficult to control how your colleagues act. (Keep in mind, you try to shoot for this behavior at all times—rehearsal, pep bands, football games, etc.) The problem usually comes after the awards because the ceremony was either exciting or a letdown. Just remember, people are always watching you and your band. How do you want your band to be perceived?

In my program, we are advised not to react no matter how the results come out. When we won our state competition, we did not react: we stood in set position until it was time to leave. When we lost at our first competition this past season, again, we did not react. We can celebrate or mourn once we are on the buses.

Need for Competitions
- Wireless microphone
- Long Ranger
- Gock block
- Drumstick


Question: How do you want others to look at your band? What do you want them saying about your band when you're not around?

# CHAPTER 4: THE TECHNICAL STUFF

## Your Score

You should be studying your score all of the time. The whole thing needs to be memorized before the band even has the music in their hands. You need to know specifics. When do the baritones come in, in part three? When does the drum line enter in part four? In what measures do the pit have their sixteenth-note run? Break down the music and know what to anticipate

This past year, I highlighted important accents that I needed to emphasize in my conducting, on my score. I also highlighted where different instruments came in. I darkened dynamics, and I wrote down different conducting gestures I could give at certain points in the music.

If you sit down and listen to the battery while watching your score, it is much easier to memorize it. You can sing along in your head with the battery; later on, this will benefit you immensely, especially in different segments at rehearsal. *The drum line and drum major relationship can make or break a band during a show.* By listening to their part while watching your score, you are setting up a strong foundation for the future, which is imperative for success.

# The Famous DM Cheat Sheet

The cheat sheet is a tool to help you memorize where certain parts of the marching music lines up with the drill. It is also there to make your life easier when you have to call out a set to the band. *Immediately after receiving new drill, you need to write the set numbers on your score!* This will help you with your cheat sheet. Here is an example of how I would set up my cheat sheet...

| Set# | # of measures | Time signature | specific entrances | Letter | Drill |
|------|---------------|----------------|--------------------|--------|-------|
| 1    | 1-4           | 4/4            | clarinets | beat 4 | beg-A | wedge |

Do this in a *very organized way* with clearly drawn lines so when you have to tell the band a certain set number, you can find it without wasting a second. Usually the staff has key words that everyone catches on to, such as "the wedge" or "the window set." Those should always be on the cheat sheet! Put the cheat sheet in the clear outside cover of your binder or, if you don't have a cover, the first page protector.

Don't always depend on the cheat sheet, though. You never know when a staff member or director will have to borrow your binder. You should have all of the segments of the show memorized. Use the cheat sheet as a tool to help you memorize these segments.

## The Metronome

Setting the metronome is not as scary as you think it is. Just make sure it's good to go, like checking your clothes before you leave your house.
- *Always* have batteries. No exceptions!
- *Always* make sure the metronome is programmed. Most directors' biggest pet peeve when about to run a segment is hearing, "The met isn't set" or "The met broke." *Well, fix it!* Things happen, but, as I said, you have to be prepared for anything. The moments when the band is not using the met is the perfect time to make sure it's working. Waiting until the met is needed is inefficient and is a waste of time for everyone.

    During basics is the perfect time to check the metronome and all of the other technical issues that go into being a drum major. Your mind has to be going through everything that could go wrong at all times. If you plan ahead, nothing bad will ever happen—well at least 95 percent of the time.
- Make sure the Long Ranger is charging before you leave school every day. There is nothing more inconvenient to a marching band while learning drill than a dead Long Ranger.

Question: What can you do to make sure you never forget important technological items? What will your cheat sheet look like?

# CHAPTER 5: THE EMOTIONAL STUFF

## Making Mistakes

*You are human: you are going to make mistakes.* Don't sweat it. Don't think about it for more than five minutes. Instead of thinking about what you *could have done,* think about what you *will do next time*. If you let a mistake get to you, it will affect how you do your job. Don't overthink things; most of the time, after ten minutes, the directors have already forgotten that you made a mistake in the first place. Seriously, it's not a big deal: everyone makes mistakes *but* just try not to make too many, all right?

Also remember to *be professional*. If you get upset, do it in private. Take a long, deep breath in and out. You are still great at what you do and will be amazing next time. As long as you learn from your mistakes, you will continue to be more and more successful each day.

Lose your fear—it is the one thing in life that holds you back from fulfilling what you want to.

## Being a Team

It's very important that your organization (the band) be unified. However; it is even more important that your section (the drum majors) be unified. Team building starts from you. It's the same effect you gain from cleaning the band room or practicing. You are setting the example for what you want to see happen in the rest of the band.

There are going to be discrepancies between you and the others. That is inevitable. We are all entitled to our own opinion, *but* if you are going to brawl, don't do it in front of the band. This shows weakness in your section and immaturity. Talk it out in a private place away from the band—it's not their problem anyway.

You as an individual also have to let the others know if something does not feel right to you. Keeping this feeling to yourself ruins the vibe of your team and your own personal chakra.

Bringing your team closer is also very important. Make T-shirts, hang out on the weekends, meet for lunch, anything. When you know each other, tasks become easier— you know each other's tendencies, which affect everything you do in band. *Plus* band is supposed to be fun. It's not all business. Building strong friendships and creating lifelong memories that you will take with you forever is what band is about. So be nice, be open, be a team player, and have fun.

## The Drum Major Title

The drum major position is important, but that doesn't mean you are better than any other person in a leadership position—or someone who is not in a leadership position. for that matter. Everyone is equally important in making band possible. You simply have a different role. When I was a freshman, I was afraid of our drum majors. They seemed so far away from where I was, almost as if they were unreachable. My goal, and you can make it yours as well, is that I am friends with or at least approachable to everyone. I want to be able to carry on a conversation with everyone in the whole band—freshman to senior.

Strive every day to make one new friend or learn a new fact about someone. Aside from all of the logistics, of course, this is the most important task for you. Making everyone feel welcome is a huge part of being a drum major. All you have to do is say hi; it will make a huge difference.

Ride on a different bus every football game, and talk to someone new. Just because you are older does not mean you are a better person than a freshman. Just because you are a drum major doesn't mean you are better than someone in operations. Keep this in mind throughout the year. Also remember, just because you are a drum major doesn't mean you are a drum major: you need to live up to your position. It isn't all about conducting— why would I write this book if it were?

## Keeping a Positive Attitude

I get it. You could be having the worst day ever, but you always have to put on a "happy face" during rehearsal or whenever you are in front of the band. Attitude is the most contagious item known to humankind. No one wants to be around someone who is negative because it brings others down as well. Everyone is trying to reach fulfillment and happiness. When you do not live up to your expectations, you become unhappy. By focusing on the good and remembering what you have and what you have already done, you will notice yourself becoming more positive and cheerful. Plus, if you are upset, not only are you putting a black cloud over the people around you: you also won't get as much done.

If you are happy, you are creating a positive force around you that will spread to others—guaranteed! This means a happy band, and a happy band means a great rehearsal, and a great rehearsal means a happy director, and a happy director means a happy everyone. See how that all started from you? Wild, right? It's crazy but I promise it's true. When everyone is positive, it's amazing what the group can accomplish. Everything in your life is controlled by how you look at it.

Question: How will you build a strong bond with your team?

What makes you happy? List below.

Section Hangout Log

1.

2.

3.

4.

5.

6.

7.

8.

9.

10.

11.

12.

# CHAPTER 6: SETTING THE EXAMPLE

## Lead by Example

It's hard to always be on your best behavior; we are all human here. Even so, you *must*, no exceptions, make a conscious effort to be on your best behavior all of the time. Don't even make an effort—*just do it.* The moment people see you misbehaving is the moment when all of your hard work goes out the window. They follow you, they respect you, and they look up to you. Literally. Whatever you do, people will begin to do. You are a leader: set a *positive example*. You don't want freshmen learning bad actions from you because bad actions turn into bad habits.

Misbehaving also weakens the band because all of the rehearsal etiquette you have worked for goes down the drain. Anyone can come back and say, "Well, you did this!" So act how you want everyone else to act—it makes life easier. You want what you are doing now with your organization to become part of the tradition, not part of the, "what not to do" section in your band handbook.

## Facebook and Networking

You are now in charge of a huge organization. People are watching your every move, and, yes, they are probably on your Facebook page. It's just like being in person—you have to set the example. When I received this position, I stopped posting anything—maybe a status once a month and a few pictures but nothing more. You have better things to do than being on Facebook anyway. **Never post anything inappropriate**. You are supposedly the model student for the rest of your band. Here's a list of what **not to do**:

- Don't spam walls
- Don't use curse words
- If your band has its own page, don't post on it every day—*please, for the sake of everyone*
- Cyber Bullying is unacceptable
- Don't post about anything that is illegal

As far as the band Facebook page goes, only post on it if it is absolutely necessary. People, myself included, get tired of getting notifications from the same person every single day. If you are a DM, posting continuously is even worse because then people really won't want to listen to you in person. This leads me to my next section.

**Speaking with Fewer Words**

"Wise men speak because they have something to say; fools because they have to say something."

—Plato

The less you speak, the more your words are worth. Don't allow people to get sick of your voice—make announcements only when absolutely necessary. There is no need to constantly yell at people. In fact, instead of yelling causing the members to do the right thing, it becomes funny to them—to the point where they will do the wrong thing on purpose just to watch you react. Don't allow that to happen in your program. It doesn't even have to be telling people when they are doing something wrong. It can be making too many announcements too.

*Never overstep the director.* The director knows what he or she is doing. Also, *don't interrupt* with an announcement that you think he or she will forget. Either the director won't forget and your interruption will be annoying, or if he or she forgets, you can *wait to make your announcement*. (Common sense, people, common sense.) The same courtesy applies with the DM tech (if you have one) or any tech. He or she is trying to help you; don't talk back and don't explain what's wrong. He or she has way more experience than you have and knows what is best for you and your DM team. If you think the tech is wrong, simply nod your head and agree and ask about it later. *Listen to the people in charge of you.*

## How to Clean a Band Room 101

You lead by example—if you begin to clean the band room and treat it well, others will acknowledge that and do the same.

- If you see a piece of trash, throw it away.
- If you see someone's property, put it in the lost and found.
- Get the correct number of chairs in each row with the correct number of stands.
- Make the rows of the chairs pretty and even.
- Make stand prongs uniform—in my band, two face you, one faces the podium.
- If you have at least six people, this should take under 3 minutes. (Delegate)

Question: What tasks can do to set a positive example daily?

1.


2.


3.


4.

5.

6.

7.

8.

9.

10.

# CHAPTER 7: YOUR DIRECTORS

There are some things you should know about your directors if you want to understand why their priorities can be different from yours:

- They get about 155 e-mails a day (this isn't an exaggeration and might be low).
- When they're attempting to respond to the e-mail they receive, students constantly interrupt them.
- They always want to help you out, but can't all of the time.
- They have to fill out a lot of paperwork to keep the band running.
- They have to eat lunch in between classes because they don't have time to eat during their actual lunchtime.
- They are band directors not miracle workers
- They have to memorize scores.
- They give private lessons in their free time.
- They often have a family to take care of, too.
- They really care about what they are doing and want the best for every single one of their students.

One of your jobs throughout the year is to make sure they don't go insane, while also not going insane in making sure they don't go insane. Still sane?

# CHAPTER 8: POST-MARCHING SEASON

You are at the top of the band food chain as a drum major. Again, you have to set the example. It starts with you. When people see you working hard, they are going to want to help you out and work hard as well. Whenever help is needed, you *have* to be there. It is your job. You shouldn't dread helping out. If you dread it, why are you here? During the year, you should ask your directors if they need any assistance...and they *always* will. They are the hardest-working, busiest people ever—understand that.

## Off-season Activities to Do

- If your program has a winter guard, be on the floor crew for anything they need help with.
- Join a winter guard or indoor percussion circuit.
- Support the winter guard! You should be at as many competitions as possible!
- The same goes for indoor percussion.
- Our school hosts the all-county band— yes, you set up the chairs, clean the facility, make sure the refrigerator is stocked with water, and lock up at the end of every rehearsal night.
- Participate in solo and ensemble.

- Ask directors if they need assistance with anything *every day.*
- Help with winter guard floor transportation for their rehearsals.
- Maintain a professional facility—get other members to help you clean the storage room, locker room, and band room if they start looking bad.
- Offer assistance to anyone who needs help with music.
- Provide private lessons on your instrument.
- For all events, you must stay late to lock up and clean the facility.
- Practice your instrument—set the example.
- Keep up with your grades in your academic classes.
- Plan for the upcoming season—review your past work and decide what to do and what not to do again.
- Recruit from middle school bands!
- Start building strong bonds with the freshman of this current band; they are the future, and you will need them next year. (It is really handy to be friends with everyone, it makes life more fun.)
- Attend all Band Booster meetings.

Question: What will you do during your off-season?

# CHAPTER 9: REMEMBER

Remember that positive energy attracts and spreads to others.

Remember that negative energy repels and spreads to others.

Remember that you are here to help.

Remember that you are responsible for your own mistakes.

Remember that you are responsible for other people's mistakes.

Remember that what you *say* is going to happen probably *will* happen.

Remember that you are human and you will make mistakes.

Remember to let go of drama, mistakes, and negative energy when you walk onto that field.

Remember you are being watched.

Remember to lead by example.

Remember to have fun. You are here for a reason.

Remember to be relentless in rehearsal and everyone's best friend outside of rehearsal.

Remember to trust yourself.

## TIPS

- Set goals for yourself. Write them on a piece of paper and hang them on the wall in your room. Check them off as you meet them.
- To keep your gloves on while conducting, purchase white sweatbands for your wrists.
- Write a list of what you need for rehearsal and for football games on your bathroom mirror with a dry erase marker.
- Use the loader tray on the copy machine if available to copy drill and music—it's faster.
- Always talk about the other person when talking to someone; don't talk about yourself unless asked a question.
- Think of this position as a game called "Making the right choice" or "What did the director say?"
- E-mail other DMs from other high schools to learn from a different outlook.
- Practice conducting in front of a mirror constantly. Record yourself and take notes. Repeat until satisfied (which should never happen).
- At rehearsal, clear your mind. You are there for the next four hours: you might as well contribute everything you have instead of stressing out about the research paper you have to write.

- Keep a journal to track your band's and your personal progress.

## REALLY GREAT QUOTES

"Luck happens when opportunity encounters the prepared mind."
*—Denis Waitley*

"The most effective way to do it, is to do it."
*—Amelia Earhart*

"Today, I am better than I was yesterday."
*—Unknown*

"What you are afraid to do, is a clear indication of what you should do next."
*—Unknown*

"Whenever you fall, pick something up."
*—Oswald Avery*

"Do not rehearse a performance, perform a rehearsal."
*—Halei Jo Fuller*

"It's a funny thing about life—if you refuse to accept anything but the best, you very often get it."
*—William Somerset Maugham*

"The reward for a thing well done, is to have it done."
*—Ralph Waldo Emerson*

"To be absolutely sure about something, you have to know everything or nothing about it."

*—Unknown*

"Silence is a friend who will never betray."

*—Confucius*

"The dumbest people I know are those who know it all."

*—Malcolm Forbes*

"Whether you think you can or can't, you're right."

*—Henry Ford*

"A real leader faces the music, even when one does not like the tune."

*—Unknown*

"When you are always ahead of others, you are always walking alone."

*—Unknown*

"The impossible—what nobody can do, until somebody does."

*—Unknown*

"Everything comes out right in the end, and if it doesn't, go left."

*—Unknown*

Made in the USA
San Bernardino, CA
03 February 2020